ARMY PROFESSIONAL EXPERTISE AND JURISDICTIONS

Richard A. Lacquement, Jr.

October 2003

FOREWORD

With the soldiers of the Army deployed to over 120 countries and executing a wide variety of missions, the Army as a profession is being stretched to its limits. Richard Lacquement takes note of these developments and calls for a clarification of what exactly the Army "profession" entails.

His mapping of the profession's expert knowledge provides a framework to continue the debate on the jurisdictions of the Army profession. The recommendations he presents are radical and thought provoking. While there may not be a consensus on his conclusions, this monograph serves the important role of stimulating thought and debate on the Army profession.

DOUGLAS C. LOVELACE, JR.
Director
Strategic Studies Institute

BIOGRAPHICAL SKETCH OF THE AUTHOR

RICHARD A. LACQUEMENT, JR., a lieutenant colonel in the U.S. Army, is a professor of Strategy and Policy at the U.S. Naval War College. He is a strategic plans and policy officer who has served in a variety of command and staff positions in both heavy and light field artillery units. Lieutenant Colonel Lacquement's artillery assignments included the 82nd Airborne Division, the 1st Armored Division (to include combat service in Operation DESERT STORM), the 3rd Infantry Division (Mechanized) and the 101st Airborne Division, (Air Assault). During Operation IRAQI FREEDOM, he served as head of the Army G3's War Plans Division's Stability Operations Planning Cell and then returned to the 101st Airborne Division to assist with stability operations in Northern Iraq. Lieutenant Colonel Lacquement has also served as an Assistant Professor of Social Sciences at the United States Military Academy where he taught courses in American politics, international relations theory, and international organizations. He is the author of *Shaping American Military Capabilities After the Cold War* (Praeger, 2003). Lieutenant Colonel Lacquement is a graduate of the U.S. Military Academy and holds master's degrees from Princeton University and the Naval War College and a Ph.D. in International Relations from Princeton University.

SUMMARY

Changes in the international security environment and in technology challenge leaders to define the Army's role for the future. Effective strategic leadership of the Army profession will be an essential component of successful transformation. To serve American society effectively, strategic leaders of the profession must define, prioritize, and limit the expert knowledge of the profession clarify the jurisdictions within which this knowledge applies, and then develop professionals to apply this knowledge.

There are three main reasons to map and prioritize the Army's professional expertise and jurisdictions:

- Facilitate choices about the use of constrained resources;
- Reestablish the Army's collective professional identity; and,
- Move beyond the concept of "full spectrum dominance."

This monograph provides a framework intended for use by the Army's strategic leaders. But it also should be a point of departure for debate among all members of the profession. The most important purpose of this framework is to provide a mechanism for HOW TO THINK about Army expert knowledge and jurisdictions. This monograph offers some general recommendations derived from my application of the framework and its logic. These recommendations represent just one possible view. Ultimately, the strategic leaders of the Army will decide priorities and boundaries.

Recommendations include:

- Eliminating of combat service support branches as basic branches for commissioned officer accession.
- Strengthening precommissioning standards for combat and combat support officers to include certified military training and educational components.
- Establishing clearer qualitative standards for assignment, promotion, and retention of commissioned officers (in terms of physical capacity, psychological capacity, and demonstrated performance).
- Refocusing the officer career management and education system.

- Developing coherent intellectual justifications and defense of jurisdictions related to the leadership of Army soldiers in the organized application of coercive force (war, peace enforcement, peacekeeping).
- Better articulating reasons for avoiding jurisdictions that do not require unique Army expertise (humanitarian assistance, disaster relief, homeland security).

ARMY PROFESSIONAL EXPERTISE AND JURISDICTION

Introduction.

> Our nonnegotiable contract with the American people is to fight and win the nation's wars. Every other task is subordinate to that commitment. To discharge our responsibilities to the Nation, we maintain several core competencies. These are the essential and enduring capabilities of our service. They encompass the full range of military operations across the spectrum of conflict, from sustained land dominance in wartime to supporting civil authorities during natural disasters and consequence management.[1]
>
> *Field Manual 1, The Army*, June 14, 2001

This quote from *Field Manual (FM) 1*, the Army's capstone manual, declares broad and compelling responsibilities for the Army. Aside from the priority for warfighting, however, it provides an undifferentiated and almost limitless range of operations for which the Army must prepare. This is a noble aspiration that reflects the best "can-do" spirit of loyal service to the nation. It is, however, a problematic practical foundation that obscures significant limitations and trade-offs required to concentrate the army's finite resources—personnel, material, and funds—on the most important requirements. Changes in the international security environment and in technology challenge leaders to define the Army's role for the future. Effective strategic leadership of the Army profession will be an essential component of successful transformation. To serve American society effectively, strategic leaders of the profession must define, prioritize, and limit the expert knowledge of the profession, clarify the jurisdictions within which this knowledge applies, and then develop the professionals to apply this knowledge.

This framework is intended for use by the Army's strategic leaders. It is also a framework for debate among all members of the profession. I hope it will generate an institutional exchange of ideas that can lead to renewed consensus on the Army's professional essence.

Problem.

> The Army needs to redraw the map of its expert knowledge and then inform and reform its educational and developmental systems accordingly, resolving any debate over the appropriate expertise of America's Army.[2]

> The Army faces increasing jurisdictional competitions with new competitors. Thus its jurisdictional boundaries must be constantly negotiated and clarified by officers comfortable at the bargaining table and skilled in dealing with professional colleagues on matters touching the profession's civil-military and political-military boundaries.[3]

The Army is at a crossroads. Its traditions, recent successes, and capabilities are praiseworthy. Its appropriate focus for the future is uncertain. "Full Spectrum Dominance" is a great bumper sticker, but of limited practical utility. It glosses over too much. It lacks boundaries. It lacks priorities.

In some ways, the tremendous success of the Army in recovering from Vietnam and better preparing for the Soviet challenge is impeding the current transformation. Clear focus on a specific foe, in a specific theater, provided a high degree of professional certainty for the Army. The "training revolution" of the 1970s led to a dramatic improvement of Army training for fighting the Soviet Union.[4] Collective and individual training were predicated on a clear overarching mission.

The current era is one of broader and less certain missions. Operation DESERT STORM drew heavily on the focused training for conventional warfare with the Soviets that characterized the Cold War. This mission fit the Army's preferred concept of war and was well-suited to its expertise developed in the latter stages of the Cold War. In contrast, numerous peace operations such as the missions in Somalia, Haiti, Bosnia, and Kosovo were not well-suited to the training and organization of the Cold War configured Army. Although still too early to draw clear lessons from the war with Iraq, success in conventional combat and difficulties in some aspects of unconventional warfare and post-conflict stabilization indicate a persistent tension about appropriate Army missions. There have been debates and significant dissonance among Army leaders between the expectations and requirements related to being prepared to "fight and win our nations wars," and the numerous operational requirements for military operations other than war (MOOTW).[5] Surveys of Army personnel and anecdotal evidence have identified related tensions within the officer corps--particularly between senior officers and junior officers.[6] Army leaders should not allow internal tensions concerning professional jurisdictions and expertise to continue.

Intellectual Foundations.

This monograph builds on two concepts. The first is the concept of the military profession provided in Samuel Huntington's classic, *The Soldier and the State.*[7] Second is the concept of professional adaptation and adjustment suggested by Andrew Abbott in *The System of Professions.*[8] Huntington provides a commonly understood definition of the military profession. With some adjustments and refinement, this monograph suggests a revised foundational definition of the Army profession. Abbott provides a framework for understanding how professions adapt and sustain themselves by defining and negotiating their roles with their clients while competing with other professions.

Huntington's definition of a profession is "a peculiar type of functional group with highly specialized characteristics."[9] To him, it is defined by expertise, responsibility, and corporateness.[10] With regard to the military profession, "The direction, operation and control of a human organization whose primary function is the application of violence is the peculiar skill of the officer."[11] The responsibility of a profession is to its client. "The military profession is monopolized by the state. The skill of the officer is the management of violence; his responsibility is the military security of his client, society."[12]

The Army professional core is found among its officers. They are required to master a body of abstract professional knowledge and understand the moral, ethical, political, and social contexts within which military actions take place. They must be experts, first and foremost, in the human dimensions--leadership, morale, and physical capacity—that underlie effective military operations.[13]

Refined to reflect this quintessentially human endeavor, the core expertise of American officers can be restated as follows. **The peculiar skill of the military officer is the development, operation, and leadership of a human organization, a profession, whose primary expertise is the application of coercive force on behalf of the American people; for the Army officer such development, operation, and leadership occurs incident to sustaining America's dominance in land warfare.** In abbreviated form, I will refer to this core expertise as **"Leadership of Army soldiers in the organized application of coercive force."**[14]

Huntington also suggested that the most appropriate means to attain effective military subordination was to maintain a clear divide between the realms of civilian and military responsibility.[15] A common critique of Huntington is that the clarity of this separation is easy to stipulate in theory but hard to realize in practice. As Clausewitz's insight suggests, since war is merely an instrument of policy, it is difficult to separate the purely military from the purely political.[16] To validate the importance of military advice, there should be standards to help determine appropriate boundaries. Defining professional expertise and jurisdictions more clearly will assist in making these distinctions.

Andrew Abbott identifies a key property of professions. Professions compete with each other to determine legitimate realms within which to apply their expertise.[17] Abbott defines professions as "somewhat exclusive groups of individuals applying somewhat abstract knowledge to particular cases."[18] Professions provide social goods to address important problems. "The tasks of professions are human problems amenable to expert service."[19] "The central phenomenon of professional life is thus the link between a profession and its work, a link [called] jurisdiction."[20] Professions compete for jurisdictions and may not always be able to claim complete control over all jurisdictions within which they compete. "Every profession aims for a heartland of work over which it has complete, legally established control." However, since full control is not always possible, there are other possible settlements. In addition to full control, jurisdictional settlements can be divided (shared with another profession), intellectual (cognitive control of a jurisdiction while allowing practical work to be widely shared), advisory (over certain aspects of work within a jurisdiction), or subordinate (another profession controls the jurisdiction, but the first profession may still do practical work within the jurisdiction).[21]

The central questions of this monograph are fundamental ones that Army leaders must address in defining the Army profession:

- What is the nature of Army expert knowledge? How should relevant expertise be prioritized?
- What are the jurisdictions within which this expertise may be legitimately applied? How should jurisdictions be prioritized? Which should be claimed and defended? Which should be avoided?

These are iterative questions that leaders of the profession must constantly address. The questions yield descriptive answers for the present and suggestive answers for the future. Strategic leaders of the Army profession must negotiate the answers with the civilian leaders who act as agents for American society. Hence, this is an important aspect of civil-military relations.

Ultimately, civilian leaders decide the Army's jurisdictions. But Army strategic leaders must represent the profession in this decisionmaking process. Civilian leaders' decisions become part of the process that requires strategic leaders of the profession to reevaluate and modify conceptions of expert knowledge and jurisdiction.

This monograph is explicitly focused on the profession as defined by the commissioned officer corps.[22] This is not meant to slight warrant officers, noncommissioned officers, or junior enlisted soldiers. These highly-skilled workers are the experts in the numerous necessary tasks that allow the Army to succeed. But the nature of their responsibilities is fundamentally different from those of the Army's commissioned officers. These soldiers and their tremendous skills are the instruments of Army success. The diagnoses, inferences, and treatments of societal problems for which these skills are appropriately applied are the responsibilities of the commissioned officers who are guardians of the profession's and the institution's essence.

The framework provided is also applicable to officers of all components of the Total Army (active, reserve, and National Guard).

With respect to the National Guard, the dynamic of jurisdictional definition and negotiation is complicated by the dual allegiance to national and state leaders. The negotiation may be more nuanced, but, the principles and logic are the same.

A New Framework.

The most important purpose of this monograph is to create a rigorous framework for HOW TO THINK about Army expert knowledge and jurisdictions. Three main reasons exist to map the Army's professional expertise and jurisdictions:

1. **Facilitate choices about the use of constrained resources**. We are required to make choices about the best ways to allocate the resources we acquire. A more rigorous framework will allow leaders to better articulate the Army's needs, in priority, on firm professional grounds.

2. **Reestablish the Army's collective professional identity.** Institutional discourse on these issues can lead to consensus about the Army profession and the role it plays for society. It can also clarify individual self-concepts of our professionals.

3. **Move beyond the concept of "full spectrum dominance."** The spectrum of conflict and range of military operations is vast. We already acknowledge that fighting and winning our nation's wars is the highest priority. Taking this as the start point, we can identify other priorities at the nexus of established expertise and possible jurisdictions. We should be forthright in debating and negotiating these priorities. We owe society and the profession improved clarity as a step towards greater effectiveness.

Defining the Army Profession's Expert Knowledge.

> Our unique contribution to national security is prompt, sustained land dominance across the range of military operations and spectrum of conflict. The Army provides the land force dominance essential to shaping the international security environment.[23]
>
> *FM 1, The Army*, June 2001

Andrew Abbott's valuable insight in the *System of Professions* is the dynamic competition among experts to command jurisdictions of practice legitimized by society. Professions succeed or fail to the degree that they provide expertise that clients need. Many professions compete in market, consumer-driven environments. The Army profession exists within a similar competitive realm; however, American society is the sole client of the Army. The Army's legitimacy and effectiveness are measured entirely in relation to meeting American society's demands for defense and security.

The suggested map of the Army profession is an effort to portray what is unique about the Army and its expertise. It also suggests how such expertise is related to society. Four broad categories of expertise are required by the Army:

1. **Military-technical expertise.** This is the Army's core expertise. "How the profession prepares for and conducts land operations combining Army soldiers with organizations, doctrine, and technology."[24] This requires the mastery of violent means to accomplish policy ends.

2. **Human development expertise.** "The Army's management of its human resources . . ."[25] and "creating, developing, and maintaining expert knowledge, and embedding that knowledge in members of the profession."[26] This expertise includes how to maximize the effectiveness of the Army's people. This also includes professional development and understanding academic fields relevant to Army training and education.

3. **Moral-Ethical expertise.** This expertise concerns the nature of professional moral duties—to members of the institution and to society. "The nature of the profession is such that only moral soldiers can discharge their professional duties, and the Army's strategic leaders are morally obligated to the client to maintain a profession of both competence and character."[27] This includes the understanding of how to apply coercive force ethically and the ethics that govern the appropriate relationship of military professionals to society (civil-military relations).

4. **Political-Social expertise.** "The Army profession serves its collective client, the American people, through interactions with the citizenry's elected and appointed leaders and the nation's other government agencies."[28] Army leaders require expertise to manage

interaction between the Army and the broader defense community (public, industry, government). This includes the critical task of representing the profession to society and advising society on the use of the profession's expertise.[29]

Table 1 provides an institutional perspective on the relevant elements of the profession's expert knowledge. They are identified by their applicability to the Army's core expertise in the leadership of Army soldiers in organized application of coercive force, especially sustained land warfare, on behalf of society. This is the heartland of the Army's abstract, expert knowledge to which all other expertise relates. The five columns assist in classifying and prioritizing areas of Army relevant expertise.

Ia. Army lead: Army has lead, if not unique, expertise. The ability to succeed in sustained land warfare is the core, indisputable responsibility of the Army. The Army cannot delegate this responsibility. Expertise in these areas differs from other military services by the relationship to sustained land warfare.

Ib. Military unique: These are areas of expertise that encompass the Army and at least one other military service. This relates the unique expertise of the Army to the other American military services (joint operations) and American allies (combined operations) on behalf of American society.

II. Army-Specific application (societal availability): Areas of expert knowledge that have counterparts within the broader society, however, within the Army, the application of this expertise requiresan important and unique adaptation. For example, medicine is a body of expert knowledge required by society as a whole. The Army has a requirement for adaptation, specialization and regulation of this expertise to the demands of Army operations—especially combat. The adaptation requires additional training or schooling. Regulating ethical application of such expertise justifies integrating individual experts in these areas directly into the Army.

III. General Application (needed internally). These are areas where society and military applications are the same. The key distinction is that the Army has routine or frequently recurring need of this expertise and of the individuals who can apply this knowledge for the Army's interests. When extensive familiarity with the Army's operations, norms, and values is important to the appropriate

	Expertise Applicability and priority →	Ia. Army Lead	Ib. Military unique	II. Army specific application	III. General application (needed internally)	IV. General application (needed externally)
	Character of expertise →	Core	Core	Core support	Acquired	Borrowed
	How Acquired →	Army Exclusive	Military Exclusive	Army and Society	Contract IN	Contract OUT
	Developmental responsibility →	Army	Military	Society with Army component	Society with Army quality control	Society
	Certification →	Army	Military	Army	Army & Society	Society
Military Technical Expert Knowledge	Leadership of Human organizations in application of coercive force	X (sustained land warfare)	X (general warfare)			
	Combat	X				
	Combat support	X				
	Joint opns		X			
	Combined opns		X			
	Admin/Logistics			X		
	Engineering/Science			X		
	Info Technology			X		
Human Development Expert Knowledge	Leadership			X		
	Human Behavior			X		
	Physical Fitness			X		
	Education			X		
	Combat Medicine			X		
	Family Medicine				X	
	Social Work				X	
Moral-Ethical Expert Knowledge	Ethical Standards	X	X			
	Character development	X	X			
	Legal			X		
	Soldier spirituality				X	
Political Social Expert Knowledge	Advice on behalf of and representation of the Profession	X	X			
	Political negotiation			X		
	Diplomacy (attaché)			X		
	Resource Acquisition & Management				X	X
Other	Basic Research					X

Table 1. Map of the Army Profession's Expert Knowledge.

exercise of such expertise on the Army's behalf, individual experts in these areas may be developed among members of the profession. To the degree that such familiarity is less crucial, experts can be hired from civilian society to apply the expertise on behalf of the Army. The exercise of expertise in these areas often involves a combination of Army professionals and civilian experts. The Army professionals in these areas provide the valuable capacity to lead, conduct liaison, and translate an area of general expertise to Army purposes. Non-Army experts in these areas are contracted into the organization.

IV. General Applications (needed externally). The last column reflects areas of expertise in society that may be borrowed and applied by non-Army professionals as needs arise and without the more demanding social and ethical controls created by integrating such practitioners directly into the Army. If expertise is available to be borrowed, there is no need to integrate it internally. Such experts can be contracted out.

Other relevant aspects of expertise include where the expertise is applied, where it should be acquired, and how it is applied.

Where applied? If practitioners in an area of expertise must be readily available within combat zones, the Army has good reasons to exercise horizontal integration to include such expertise within the organization. In these cases, the expectation of operating in a violent environment is a key consideration (e.g., medics, chaplains, drivers, pilots). If the expertise doesn't need to be applied in a combat zone, there may be no need for it inside the Army.

Where acquired? Who controls the life cycle of expertise development and educational advancement? For Army lead/dominant expertise, the Army should be responsible for the entire life cycle of expertise development and application. For expertise created elsewhere in society, but with specific Army applications, the Army is responsible for developing the capacity for Army-specific aspects. For expertise with general applications in society, the Army should leave training and development to others but must ensure quality control in application to Army purposes.

How applied? Is there a particular ethical or moral element peculiar to its Army application? This implies an important component of ethical control that differs from society more generally. A good example would be application of information technology as a form of warfare (to hurt, kill or disable others through effects on societal infrastructure or other public goods).

Defining the Expert Knowledge of Individual Professionals.

> The quality, maturity, experience, and intellectual development of Army leaders and Soldiers become even more critical in handling the broader range of simultaneous missions in this complex [future] operational environment.[30]
>
> U.S. Army Objective Force White Paper 2001

The previous section provided a framework for understanding the areas of expert knowledge required by the Army at an institutional level. The combination of numerous professionals with diverse paths of development and integration provide the aggregate pool of expertise to serve the profession. The next step is to suggest a map of the expertise of individual Army professionals.

Future challenges will place high demands on new officers.

> Officers of the 21st Century must be flexible, principled, and self-learning. These officers will be challenged to lead American soldiers and make complex decisions in complicated environments with little or no time. They will be part Harvard professor, part professional athlete, part Ambassador, and all disciplined warfighter. It will take each one of these attributes to be successful on the 21st Century battlefield.[31]

This is a tall order for each officer. The Army as a profession needs the expertise of professors, athletes, ambassadors, and warfighters. The degree to which each professional must possess all this expertise is an important consideration. This section suggests a framework to understand the appropriate relationship of the profession's general requirements and the manner in which individuals develop expertise to meet the profession's specific demands. It suggests a framework for professional expertise appropriate to both generalists and specialists. It recognizes that members of the profession cannot all be masters of every area of expert knowledge required by the Army as an institution.

The Army seeks to create generalists *familiar* with many or all of the major aspects of the profession's expertise and the appropriate use of such expertise in complementary, synergistic combination. These generalists are the core from which we obtain the strategic leaders of the profession. Complementing these generalists are the specialists who *master* areas of knowledge that support the Army's success in its core expertise. Specialists serve the profession through high level expertise in a particular field akin to the Harvard professors, professional athletes, and ambassadors.

> The ambiguous nature of the operational environment requires Army leaders who are self-aware and adaptive. Self-aware leaders understand their operational environment, can assess their own capabilities, determine their own strengths and weaknesses, and actively learn to overcome their weaknesses. Adaptive leaders must first be self-aware—then have the additional ability to recognize change in their operating environment, identify those changes, and learn how to adapt to succeed in their new environment.[32]

The schools and assignment process must be designed to nurture these traits over time so that it creates the foundation of professional expertise at higher levels. Familiarity with the higher level concepts among junior members of the profession also ensures that they understand the context of decisions and guidance.

The relative demand for education versus training should increase as officers rise in rank and experience. Mastery of specific skills and tasks should give way to broader theoretical and conceptual training. This is a means to greater flexibility, versatility, psychological maturity, and mental agility. This also corresponds to the higher levels of uncertainty and greater opportunities for choice that accompany promotion and commensurately higher professional responsibilities.

Precommissioning must address all elements of the Army's expertise and jurisdiction as candidly as possible with rising officers. All officers should have the same foundations of professional ethics, understanding of officership, and the intellectual seasoning of a broad but balanced technical-scientific and humanities education. Core military programs and supporting academic programs are designed to work in tandem. The academic program provides a broad context for expertise appropriate to the Army profession. The core military program reinforces these elements with Army or military specific academic courses, practical experience, and rigorous training. Success in this comprehensive program permits the profession to certify that its new members have an acceptable foundation for a career of principled service to the nation. The functional imperatives of the profession require that its commissioned leaders have the mental agility to recognize problems and draw on a complex body of knowledge to suggest appropriate diagnoses, inferences and treatments.

This program should be standardized across all commissioning sources. Large portions of the military program are already standardized.[33] The academic requirements to support Army professional expertise are less consistent. A bachelor's degree generally is considered sufficient to meet professional academic qualification from Reserve Officer Training Corps (ROTC) programs. For Officer Candidate School (OCS), a bachelor's degree is not required before commissioning, but must be attained before attending the Captain's Career Course.[34] For ROTC and OCS, the specific components of the academic program are largely at the individual's discretion.[35] Precommissioning academic requirements should be better standardized to meet Army professional needs.

The body of relevant knowledge that affects the Army's ability to function effectively has increased dramatically over time. Masters of particular fields require specialization and long-term experience. Table 2 illustrates specialties currently identified by the Army as they relate to the categories of Army expertise.

Table 2 depicts several important concepts. First, all Army professionals enter through the box in the lower left hand corner. That is the area representing the operational force (combat and combat support). Ultimately, the operational force will generate the aptly named general officers who will lead the profession. Medical, legal, and religious experts are acquired from their appropriate professional education systems. Additional orientation or training occurs to integrate these non-Army professionals into the institution.

The arrows with their origins in the lower left box represent the OPMS III mid-career specialization tracks that draw on officers who have a strong professional foundation in the operational force.

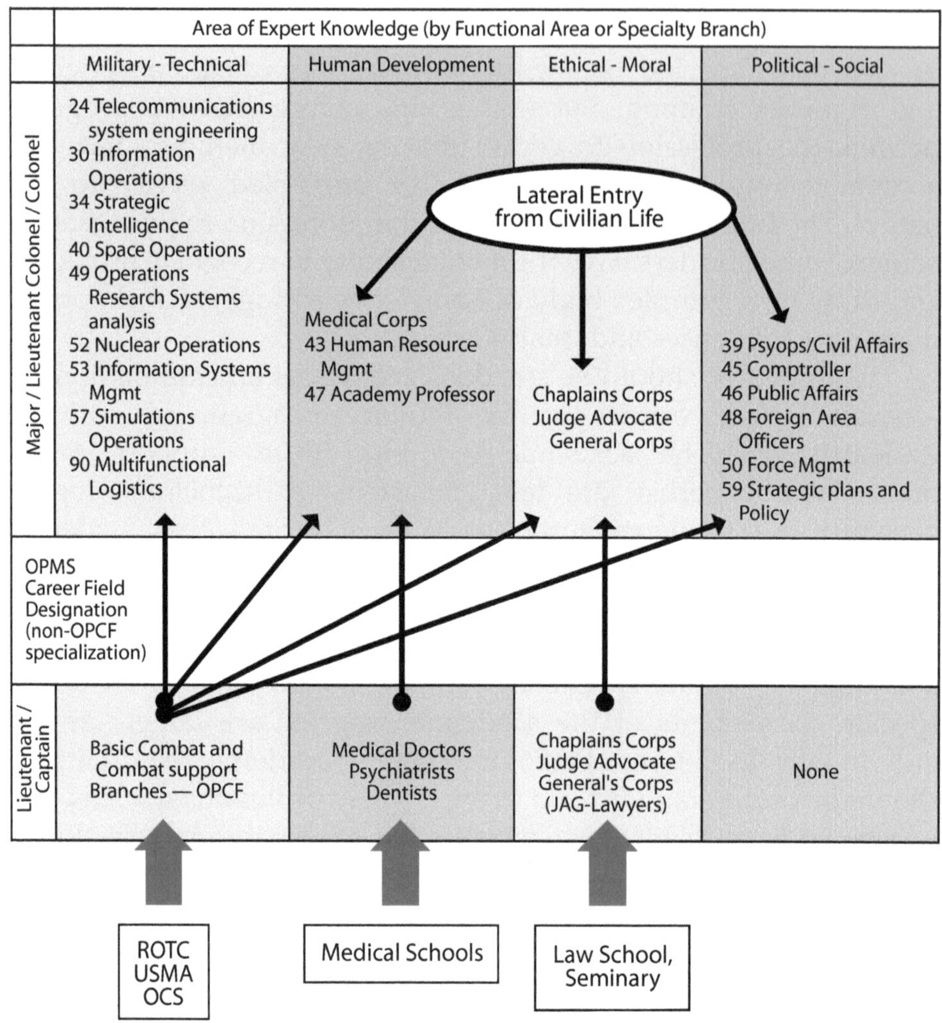

Table 2. Nonoperations Career Field (OPCF) Specialization.

Table 2 depicts the idea that there are specialists in the civilian world whose expertise can serve the Army's needs. Specialties that are not unique to the Army lend themselves to lateral entry. Examples include civilian professors within the Army School system, public affairs experts, comptrollers, and systems analysts. The argument for including Army professionals with significant combat and combat support experience in these specialties rests heavily on the degree that such experience is necessary to integrate this knowledge to the Army's requirements.

Map of Professional Expertise: Practical Implications and Applications.

The priority expertise of the Army profession is the human dimension of leadership. The Army is most importantly about its people and their ability to apply their skills in a potentially violent environment to serve American society. The abstract knowledge of leadership, particularly for combat, must dominate the Army's professional essence.

Knowledge of technology, military doctrine, human development, professional ethics, and political-social context supports the quintessential focus on the leadership of human organizations to achieve appropriate military effects.

The focus of the Army profession on the leadership of soldiers in the organized application of coercive force suggests a few important ways to rethink the structure and composition of the officer corps.

Elimination of Combat Service Support Branches for Officer Accession.

These branches have no peculiar or unique skill related to leadership of Army soldiers in the organized application of coercive force. Instead, these skills can be provided through functional area specialization and civilian contracts at higher level. Within tactical units, combat service support task execution can be allocated to Warrant Officers and NCOs. Service support elements should be integrated into existing combat and combat support units where the commissioned officers provide the most important professional skill--leadership. Command and staff assignments should be allocated to combat and combat support officers. The practical result is the elimination of finance, adjutant general, quartermaster, transportation, and ordnance as officer accession branches.

Realignment of Precommissioning System.

Precommissioning programs should better distinguish between officer candidates for operational force basic branches and candidates for special branches (medical, legal, chaplain, etc.).[36] Operational force officers should have the same educational foundations. This should include common core military programs and common core academic requirements. Eligibility for accession to combat and combat support branches should require Army *certified* completion of the military core program and a baccalaureate degree that includes Army-specified elements. Additionally, Army sponsored programs (USMA, OCS, and ROTC scholarships) should require accession to basic branches (combat and combat arms). Transfer to special branches (medical, legal, religious) should be permitted only after an initial service obligation in basic branches has been met.[37]

Establish Stronger Qualitative Standards for Promotion and Advancement.

Initial certification of professional competence should be augmented with periodic professional certification for advancement. This is an important element in making sure that qualitative professional standards dominate. Providing aggregate numbers of personnel should be a subordinate objective. We know and can establish appropriate qualifications for a particular rank and responsibility.

Psychological development models have recognized that certain stages of development are better suited for particular positions.[38] To identify the appropriate position of a particular individual at a point in their life is difficult but not impossible. The ability to measure and code a person's stage of psychological maturity would require substantially different evaluation tools, but it can be done.

Similarly, we know the physiological demands to which individuals will be subjected in various assignments. A minimal level of fitness for all soldiers makes sense in the same way the various physical disabilities and mental deficiencies are bars to entry. We know the routine as well as the extraordinary demands of particular situations. We can tailor physical fitness tests better to reflect the needs of particular specialties. This can provide objective standards that transcend charges of political correctness.

There is nothing that prevents us from establishing specialty related standards in physical fitness, mental acuity, and psychological development. Additionally, testing should be designed to accommodate personal improvement and development. Similar to programs to improve current general test (GT) scores, we should design a system for improvement and reevaluation. If the standards for entering a particular specialty are meaningful, they must also be subject to revalidation. The requirements for officers should be particularly stringent.

Career Management and Education.

Army leaders must ensure that professional values—not bureaucratic imperatives—drive the military education and assignment system. The two key elements of this structure are the Army's professional military education (PME) system and the closely related assignment patterns that shape individual professionals.

Senior military leaders are not laterally appointed from other sectors of society. They must enter at the lower ranks of the profession and advance within the boundaries of profession's assignment, education and promotion system. Through this process of professional development, the services establish and reinforce concepts of professionalism to meet the diverse and shifting challenges of an uncertain era.

This requires a professional development system that produces individuals to meet current and short run challenges and who can also adapt to uncertain future challenges. Such a system must place less emphasis on narrow technical skills that are perishable and greater emphasis on qualities of enduring value (physical, spiritual, and ethical). The system must seek to develop individuals with the capacity to learn and grow professionally throughout a lifetime of service to the nation. In an era of rapidly changing technology, mastery of particular weapons and equipment may provide only fleeting benefit. More important is the intellectual agility of leaders to understand the dynamics of change and to be able to readily adapt new capabilities to enduring requirements and old capabilities to new requirements.

Defining the Army's Professional Jurisdictions.

The Army operates in jurisdictions ultimately legitimized by the demands of society, represented by its civilian leaders. In a passive formulation, the Army is simply a loyal servant of society and does what it is asked to do. Superficially accurate and normatively supportable, this formulation overlooks an important responsibility for the profession to participate in clarifying appropriate jurisdictions in negotiation with its societal clients. The Army's professional expertise and capabilities are finite. The Army is capable of performing duties unrelated to its core expertise and core mission. The costs of doing so must be measured against its ability to perform duties effectively for which it is uniquely designed and for which society is solely reliant upon the Army. Army leaders must be able to reconcile the jurisdictions within which the profession operates with the expertise and capacity it possesses. Civilian leaders have the final decision; nonetheless, Army leaders should be clear about the nature of the Army's appropriate role in specific jurisdictions.

Expertise is developed for application within particular jurisdictions. If jurisdictions are no longer relevant to the client's needs, a profession with expertise in that area may no longer be useful. If expertise to address problems in a jurisdiction can be found elsewhere, competition may eliminate the need for a profession's particular body of abstract knowledge and, hence, lead to the profession's death.

The uncertainty and challenges of the present era provide an impetus for professional competition. Other military services, other government agencies and private organizations compete with the Army to address American society's security concerns. Many responsibilities associated with the Army have been challenged and claimed by others. Moreover, laudable service in missions that have little to do with the use of coercive force blur public understanding of the Army's core roles, thus making it easier to challenge other roles. Strategic leaders of the Army profession must recognize this dynamic, competitive context as they define the appropriate role of the Army.

The other military services challenge the Army's role to dominate land combat with claims for battlespace dominance that blur distinctions of air, sea, and land domains. Even regarding land warfare, the rapid expeditionary use of Marines challenges central claims of the Army's relevance and importance. Contracting for training of Army officers (within the ROTC program) and the training of foreign armies represent further competition in jurisdictions previously run by the Army. In a variety of MOOTW missions, Army efforts compete with international governmental and nongovernmental organizations.

The core of the Army's map of expert knowledge is the development, operation, and leadership of a human organization whose primary expertise is the application of coercive force on behalf of the American people incident to dominance in land warfare. The jurisdictions within which this expertise apply are conventional war, unconventional war, military operations other than war, and homeland security. This section briefly analyzes each jurisdiction using a framework based on Abbott's description of possible jurisdictional claim settlements.[39]

The most important settlement claim is for full and complete control of jurisdictions (FULL). Next are those jurisdictions that the Army shares with other American military services and allies (DIVIDED). The other three forms of settlement (intellectual, advisory, or subordinate) reflect lower priority jurisdictions relative to the profession's expertise. In descending order of priority, INTELLECTUAL jurisdiction is with "the dominant profession retaining only cognitive control of the jurisdiction, while allowing practical jurisdiction to be shared more widely."[40] Another settlement is to "allow one profession an ADVISORY control over certain aspects of the work."[41] Last is the concept of SUBORDINATION. In this settlement another profession (or professions) retains primary responsibility. The Army may have skills that are applicable and can therefore assist, but concedes control to other professions or agencies.[42]

The most important reason to have an Army is to support national security, and, in particular, to defend against armed forces—irregular, uniformed, foreign, or domestic—that threaten the security of the nation and it citizens. But the Army's utility and value has also been understood in a much broader context. "Essentially, the Army as a profession emerged to embrace any tasks levied by the American people that necessitated the deployment of trained, disciplined, manpower under austere conditions on behalf of the nation."[43] This broader conception of the Army's utility beyond war accounts for the extensive involvement of the Army in nation-

Jurisdiction	Settlement Claim
Conventional War	
Land War	FULL
Joint Warfare	DIVIDED
Combined Warfare	DIVIDED
Unconventional War	
Low intensity conflict/guerrilla warfare	DIVIDED
Nuclear War	ADVISORY
Military Operations Other Than War	
Peace Enforcement (ground forces)	FULL
Peacekeeping	DIVIDED
Humanitarian Assistance	SUBORDINATE
Disaster Relief/assistance	SUBORDINATE
Military-to-Military contacts (with foreign ground forces)	FULL
Homeland Security	
WMD response (chem, bio, nuke protection)	INTELLECTUAL
Law enforcement support	SUBORDINATE

Table 3. Jurisdictions and Army Settlement Claims.

building tasks at home and abroad. This includes exploration of the continent (Lewis and Clark), development of vast civil engineering works, occupation and pacification of North American territories (to include conflicts with native Americans), as well as occupation and administration of territories abroad (such as Mexico, Cuba, the Philippines, Germany, and Japan).

The most important jurisdiction of the military professions is war. The war jurisdictions are led, if not monopolized, by the military services. Leadership of people in the organized use of coercive force on behalf of the state is the special expertise of military professionals.

The increasingly intertwined effects of military operations on land, in the air, at sea, in space, and, according to many, in cyberspace, preclude clear distinctions between the domains of combat within which the military services specialize. The overlap and interplay of capabilities optimizes for air, sea, and land operations permit application in the jurisdiction of other services, albeit it with varied degrees of efficiency. This situation makes interservice competition possible. This competition is a messy but ultimately very successful mechanism for identifying, debating, and deciding issues concerning society as a whole.

The Army profession competes with the maritime profession (Navy and Marines) and the aerospace profession (Air Force) with respect to a variety of national objectives amenable to the use of force. The Army is not always sufficient or even necessary to address all challenges. The Army and other military professions offer a menu of capabilities from which American society can choose. The perception of a particular profession's utility is a function of the manner in which problems are defined, diagnosed, and suggested for treatment.

To take a conventional war example, it is not necessarily clear in advance what strategy will prove most effective in compelling an enemy to do our will. Will naval blockade be sufficient? Will air power alone be sufficient? Will it be necessary to seize and hold portions of territory? Typically, all means that can contribute to success will be applied. The issue is to determine an effective combination. More broadly, effective diplomacy (the expertise of Foreign Service professionals) can obviate the need for any military action. If there are a variety of effective combinations and permutations, assessment of relative risk and cost effectiveness will influence choices.

The manner in which competing professions define the issue will be important. For war and preparation for war, there is not likely to be one correct answer.

> Military science is not normally so exact as to rule out all but one school of thought on the question of how battles are to be fought and wars won. As a result, military planners frequently find themselves uncertain or divided regarding the kinds of

> preparations necessary to support the foreign policy purposes of the nation. There is, moreover, the additional complication that some purposes might alternatively be met through nonmilitary means, that is, through economic or diplomatic arrangements, or through the allocation of American resources to advance the military power of other nations.[44]

Each American military service differs in its dominant concept of war and the best means to carry it out.[45] In an uncharitable light, these service specific diagnoses and suggested treatments are grounded in organizational self-interest. This does not, however, mean that the professionals advancing such arguments are unpatriotic or unreasonable. They are all trying to achieve success for society. The services and their strategic leaders are responsible for articulating the appropriate ways that service capabilities best serve societal needs. This competition is a healthy one that identifies alternatives for national leaders. The services sustain or create capabilities through a variety of methods. The government does not have infinite resources and must therefore constantly reevaluate trade-offs both across and within a variety of jurisdictions. There is nothing self-evident or exclusive about the claims the Army advances concerning appropriate national strategy and appropriate resource allocation. Strategic leaders of the Army profession must clearly articulate the relevance of the Army's expertise to appropriate jurisdictions.

Society aspires to attain policy goals in the most effective manner at the least possible cost. The lack of objective criteria to determine the relative value of one course of action or combination of means versus another simply suggests that there is value to the advice of various professions' leaders to clarify the relevance and application of their profession's expertise.

For MOOTW, the unique tasks for which the military is well-suited are those that require the use or possible use of coercive force. The Army should retain full jurisdiction for such missions. The Army is configured and trained to deter or defeat threats from organized military forces.

With regard to peacekeeping, the Army has the capacity to deter or defeat paramilitary, unconventional, or guerrilla forces. Although duties may include actions similar to domestic policing activities, the situations are ones that could escalate to armed clashes. Where traditional peacekeepers or police might be rapidly overwhelmed, combat-organized Army forces provide overmatch capabilities and the potential for escalation dominance.

With regard to peacekeeping missions, military-to-military contacts, peace enforcement, humanitarian assistance, and other nonwarfighting missions, there is a strong case for the employment of the readily available and robust capabilities of the Army to undertake missions that other agencies of the U.S. Government or private organizations are unable to accomplish. For some missions, such as humanitarian assistance and disaster relief, the issue is not unique Army capabilities, but rather the speed with which the Army can respond and the ability to undertake such tasks in an austere, remote, or unsecure environment. In these situations, the valuable Army capacity is rapid response. The capacity to support such missions is an inherent part of the Army's warfighting ability. The Army is prepared for the exigencies of war to include destruction of parts of the organization in combat. Hence, military units are capable of rapidly providing infrastructure and support mechanisms. Professionally, however, these are not unique Army jurisdictions. The Army can apply its skills subordinate to civilian governmental and nongovernmental experts. These other experts should assume long-term responsibility for these tasks as soon as possible.

Defining Appropriate Jurisdictions: Practical Implications and Applications.

The Army is expected to operate effectively on behalf of national security objectives within many jurisdictions. The Army must place the greatest emphasis on those for which it should have full and complete control—those relevant to leadership of Army soldiers in the organized application of coercive force. In particular, this includes all aspects of sustained land warfare (conventional and unconventional) as well as peacekeeping and peace enforcement missions where the potential for coercive force—if not its actual use—is required. These are the Army's highest priority missions. The Army must articulate its relevant dominance of these jurisdictions and must seek to sustain its professional expertise as the lead proponent for effective performance in them.

All other jurisdictions are secondary. The common element of these is the fungible utility of Army capabilities. Professionally, the Army does not possess unique expertise in these areas. Other professions or agencies possess the expertise to lead or manage operations. The Army may possess expertise or capabilities that can be applied—but at a substantial opportunity cost.

Note that the relative priority of *professional* jurisdiction is an important distinction. There are certainly many tasks that Army units or Army individuals will be well-suited to perform in secondary jurisdictions that create minimal, if any, opportunity costs for the individuals or units involved. A more appropriate way to conceptualize this would be to note that Army capabilities may be borrowed (or lent) for application in jurisdictions outside the Army profession. Professionally, the Army's role is advisory or subordinate within these jurisdictions, and Army strategic leaders should seek to avoid accepting responsibility for them. Army leaders should, however, maintain the expertise to manage effective liaison with those individuals or professions that do control or lead these jurisdictions (political-social expertise).

Another way to look at it is that turf battles to define and control primary jurisdictions are not only warranted but required. For secondary jurisdictions, such battles should not be joined. If *conscripted* to accept such secondary jurisdictions (a distinct possibility for a profession also defined by loyal service to society) professional leaders should actively seek appropriate ways to hand off, or spin-off, the jurisdiction. If there is no way to do this, strategic leaders must explore adaptations to the profession that may involve segmenting a portion of the profession to handle the new jurisdiction while shielding the rest (e.g., the creation of specific constabulary forces for peacekeeping in benign environments).[46]

To fix problems with lack of clarity concerning appropriate jurisdictions, Army leaders must work with both the civilian policy leaders and with the junior members of the profession. With regard to these junior members, the Army's strategic leaders must articulate the multifaceted demands for Army professionals. The Army's strategic leaders must actively advise civilian leaders on how to define and clarify service jurisdictions. They cannot afford to be passive and merely accept civilian preferences. "Can-do" acquiescence is a laudable trait when tasks are clear or decisions already made. It does not require silence in shaping decisions. At the other extreme, it is also unacceptable for military leaders to insist on controlling the definition of jurisdictions. Strategic leaders must draw on their experience and their vision for the profession to advise and negotiate with civilian leaders.

Ultimately, military leaders are beholden to civilian leaders' decisions about the Army's jurisdiction. On one hand, Army leaders must ensure that the profession's leaders and soldiers are aware of the tasks society may require. Continued emphasis on the "fight and win the nation's wars" mantra must be imbedded in a larger context of service to the nation on behalf of national security objectives. War is only one, albeit the most important, professional jurisdiction. On the other hand, strategic leaders of the Army must advise civilian leaders on appropriate definition of the Army's jurisdictions and the prospective costs of shifting jurisdictions capriciously. This is necessary to help maintain a consistent core identity for the members of the profession and to sustain the institution's reliable performance. Army strategic leaders play a critical role negotiating the profession's identity at the nexus of its internally understood identity and its responsiveness to society's demands.

OBSTACLES TO CHANGE

Arguing with Success.

A significant challenge to making changes in the Army profession is the fact that there is little or no evidence of Army failure in the most important measures of Army effectiveness. This is certainly a good thing. In combat, the Army has performed very well since the end of the Vietnam War. The most dramatic examples of Army successes are Operation DESERT STORM, Operation ENDURING FREEDOM, and Operation IRAQI FREEDOM. In operations other than war, to include Somalia, Haiti, Bosnia, Kosovo, and Iraq, the Army has also performed superbly.

Past success does not guarantee future performance. As General Douglas MacArthur put it, "We must hold our minds alert . . . The next war will be won in the future, not in the past."[47] The Army should not be content to rest on its laurels. The fact that the Army has yet to fail in a manner that *requires* change is a weak excuse for not making changes that can avert failure. Adversaries constantly seek to nullify or counter our capabilities. Changes in the international environment and technology pose daunting challenges. The Army must continually validate its choices against a healthy respect for the shadow of the future. Choices now severely constrain future capabilities. This is true with regard to choices of weapon systems and equipment. It is also true with regard to the nature of recruitment, training, and development that will grow the strategic leaders of tomorrow's Army from the junior members of today's profession.

Overcoming Transaction Costs.

Many of the changes suggested in this monograph create high costs in the short run. In particular, changes contemplated for the professional development system will be very difficult. Even the most clearly justified changes must seek to mitigate problems generated by personnel turmoil, career anxiety, and social disruption. In the wake of the Cold War, one of the most commonly cited problems for the downsized force was uncertainty and anxiety about the organization's future and the effect on its members' lives.

Army strategic leaders must be able to articulate the value of changes that warrant the short-term disruptions. The short-term costs to individuals must be justified in terms of the profession's long-term effectiveness.

The Army personnel system is a successful one that has done much to render predictable the patterns of an Army career. Paths to future responsibility and success are relatively well-defined. Senior officers successful at treading these paths often reinforce the patterns of their careers in their guidance and endorsement of junior officers. Similarly, particular school and training requirements have been incorporated into the pattern of assignments to assist in the appropriate assembly of professional skills and experience. Certainly much recommends this system as an appropriate response to the demands of running a large organization efficiently. But the most important rationale for the personnel system is its effectiveness in supporting fundamental national defense. Bureaucratic structures cannot be allowed to dictate the principles of military effectiveness.

Recommendations for Further Study.

Additional study is necessary to refine the map of the profession's expert knowledge and that of individual professionals. More work is needed to create the professional development pathways for individuals. The principles that led me to suggest boundaries of the Army's expert knowledge may suggest different conclusions to others. Ultimately, specific decisions needed to operationalize this approach are the responsibility of the profession's strategic leaders.

This framework can serve is a useful point of departure for examination of subelements of the Army profession. Additional study and application by leaders of the current Army branches and functional areas would be useful to help define the expert knowledge of branches and the jurisdictions within which they should appropriately operate. The focus of this monograph is at the Army's institutional level. Greater definition will help us to better see how these principles apply to the specialties that comprise the profession. The future of the Infantry profession, Armor profession, Field Artillery profession, and other areas of Army expert knowledge would be useful adjuncts to this monograph.

Although it contains broad implications for other members of the organization (warrant officers, noncommissioned officers, junior enlisted soldiers and civilians), this monograph does not provide detailed analysis or recommendations for the transformation of these members' roles. This is an area for fruitful additional study.[48] A key aspect of such an analysis would include the manner in which warrant officer and noncommissioned officer specialization might incorporate tasks formerly expected of commissioned officers that no longer require the application of abstract professional knowledge. Restructured warrant and enlisted occupational specialties may prove an appropriate mechanism for assimilation of such skills. It may also be appropriate to restructure such tasks as part of the Army's civilian work force.

Conclusion.

Army leaders must nurture a strong, healthy relationship between the Army and the society it serves. To do this effectively, they must think strategically about the future of the profession. Strategic leaders need a clear understanding of the nature of the Army's expertise and the jurisdictions within which it can be usefully applied. Strategic leaders of the profession must negotiate jurisdictions with society's civilian leaders from the firmest possible foundation derived from what Clausewitz called "the grammar of war."[49] Military advice not derived from professional expertise compromises the legitimacy of advice in other contexts.

> Positions based on either an overly narrow or an overly broad conception of the military's professional expertise could ultimately have negative consequences. The input of military officers could come to be seen either as irrelevant to the needs of the policy-maker, or as having dubious professional credibility.[50]

Strategic leaders imperil the Army institution if they lose sight of the professional foundations of their role and allow themselves to be drawn into policy and other debates that exceed their professional expertise and experience. It is a fine line between Clausewitz's wise counsel for officers to be sensitive to the political context within which they operate and actually stepping in to try to determine appropriate policy goals. The framework presented here can help draw that line more clearly.

The security challenges of the future are complex, demanding, and uncertain. The territory may be difficult to negotiate, but many sound guidelines are available to map a successful course. The Army needs strategic leadership to determine the required expert knowledge for specific professional jurisdictions and to develop the individuals to apply this professional expertise appropriately. The Army's strategic leaders must also negotiate to bound and prioritize the profession's jurisdictions and expertise with the civilian leaders representing society. These efforts will more resolutely set the Army on a successful axis of advance to meet the nation's future security challenges.

ENDNOTES

1. *FM 1, The Army,* Washington, DC: Department of the Army, June 14, 2001, p. 32.

2. Don. M. Snider and Gayle Watkins. eds., *The Future of the Army Profession,* New York: The McGraw-Hill Companies, Inc., 2002, p. 538.

3. *Ibid.*, p. 543.

4. For a description of the training revolution of the 1970s, see Rodler F. Morris, Scott W. Lackey, George J. Mordica II, and J. Patrick Hughes, *Initial Impressions Report: Changing the Army,* Fort Leavenworth, KS: Combined Arms Center History Office, Center for Army Lessons Learned, 1994. Available from *http://call.army.mil/products/exfor/specrpt/sprptoc.htm*, Internet, accessed May 25, 2002.

5. "Executive Summary," *American Military Culture in the Twenty-First Century,* A Report of the CSIS International Security Program, Washington DC: The Center for Strategic and International Studies Press, February 2000, pp. xxii-xxiii.

6. *American Military Culture in the Twenty-First Century,* and Army Training and Leader Development Panel, *Officer Study: Report to The Army,* May 2001, available at *http://www.army.mil/features/ATLD/report.pdf,* Internet, accessed November 1, 2001; Joe LeBoeuf, "Three Case Studies on the Army's Internal Jurisdictions, Case No. 3: The 2000 Army Training and Leader Development Panel," Chapter 22, in Snider and Watkins, *Future of the Army Profession,* p. 487.

7. Samuel P. Huntington, *The Soldier and the State,* Cambridge: Harvard University Press, 1957.

8. Andrew Abbott, *The System of Professions: An Essay on the Division of Expert Labor,* Chicago: University of Chicago Press, 1988.

9. Huntington, p. 7.

10. *Ibid.*, p. 8.

11. *Ibid.*, p. 11.

12. *Ibid.*, pp. 14-15.

13. This is significantly different than the expectation of warrant officers, noncommissioned officers, and junior enlisted soldiers. In Huntington's formulation, the difference between officers and other members of the force is that officers must be experts in the management of violence whereas other members of

the organization (warrant officers, NCOs, junior enlisted soldier) must be expert in the application of violent means. Huntington, *The Soldier and the State*, p. 11.

14. I acknowledge the help of Don Snider in crafting this wording for the nature of the Army profession's core expertise. E-mail communication with the author, May 29, 2002.

15. Huntington, p. 83.

16. Carl von Clausewitz, *On War*, Princeton: Princeton University Press, 1976, p. 87.

17. Abbott, *The System of Professions*, p. 318.

18. *Ibid.*

19. *Ibid.*, p. 35.

20. *Ibid.*, p. 20.

21. *Ibid.*, pp. 69-71.

22. In this study, commissioned officers refers to officers in the rank of 2nd lieutenant and above and does not include commissioned warrant officers.

23. *FM 1*, p. 21.

24. Snider and Watkins, *The Future of the Army Profession*, p. 101.

25. *Ibid.*, p. 438.

26. *Ibid.*, p. 355.

27. *Ibid.*, p. 291.

28. *Ibid.*, p. 197.

29. Huntington, p. 72.

30. U.S. Army, *Concepts for the Objective Force*, U.S. Army White Paper, undated, p. 3.

31. William J. Lennox, Jr., "The Supe's Letter: A Soldier of the 21st Century," *Assembly*, Vol. LX, No. 4, March/April 2002, p. 8.

32. *FM 1*, p. 12.

33. For a detailed list of the common core tasks for the OES system at the company grade and precommissioning level, see *http://cgsc.leavenworth.army.mil/cal/LETDD/COMMON1.htm*, Internet, accessed May 30, 2002.

34. This happens after approximately 3 years of commissioned service. *Department of the Army Pamphlet (DA Pam) 600-3*, Paragraph 4-16b, p. 19.

35. The AR does require that ROTC scholarship candidates have an approved major. However, the list of approved majors is extremely comprehensive and appears to suggest very little restriction on acceptable academic programs. The only specific requirement listed in the AR is for one semester of language.

36. The special branches are the Judge Advocate General's Corps (legal), Chaplain Corps (religious), and Medical Corps. Medical corps includes the following six sub-elements: medical corps, dental corps, veterinary corps, Army Medical Specialists, Army Nurse Corps, and Medical Service Corps. DA Pam 600-3, Paragraph 8-2c, p. 31.

37. Service obligations are as follows. Military Academy graduates are obligated for 8 years of service, 5 of which, at a minimum, must be served on active duty. ROTC scholarship recipients incur an 8-year service obligation, of which 4 must be on active duty and the remaining 4-6 years in the reserves or National Guard (ROTC information from U.S. Army Cadet Command Headquarters, available from *http://www.rotc.monroe.army.mil/scholarships/green/obligation.asp*, Internet, accessed May 30, 2002.) OCS commissioned officers have a 3-year active duty service obligation. Date from Department of the Army, *Army Regulation 350-100: Officer Active Duty Service Obligations,* May 4, 2001, p. 5.

38. Forsythe, *et al.*, in Snider and Watkins.

39. The detailed discussion of claim settlements can be found in Abbott, pp. 69-79.

40. *Ibid.*

41. *Ibid.*, emphasis by author.

42. *Ibid.*, pp. 71-72.

43. Leonard Wong and Douglas V Johnson II, "Serving the American People: A Historical View of the Army Profession," in Snider and Watkins, eds., *The Future of the Army Profession*, New York: McGraw-Hill Primus Custom Publishers, 2002, p. 62.

44. Warner R. Schilling, "The Politics of National Defense: Fiscal 1950," in *Strategy, Politics and Defense Budgets*, 1-266, New York: Columbia University Press, 1962, p. 13.

45. For an excellent treatment of these differences, see Carl H. Builder, *The Masks of War: American Military Styles in Strategy and Analysis*, Baltimore: Johns Hopkins University Press, A RAND Corporation Research Study, 1989, especially chapter 5, pp. 57-66.

46. An historical example of this may have been those portions of the U.S. Army Corps of Engineers responsible for domestic duties such as river/flood management.

47. General Douglas MacArthur, as quoted by Lennox, p. 8.

48. As part of the Army Training and Leader Development panels, follow-on efforts to the officer study address warrant officers, noncommissioned officers, and Army civilians. The implications of this study could be used to modify the results of these other panels.

49. Clausewitz, p. 605.

50. Suzanne Neilson, "Rules of the Game? The Weinberger Doctrine and the American Use of Force," in Snider and Watkins, eds., *The Future of the Army Profession*, New York: McGraw-Hill Primus Custom Publishers, 2002, p. 219.

www.ingramcontent.com/pod-product-compliance
Ingram Content Group UK Ltd.
Pitfield, Milton Keynes, MK11 3LW, UK
UKHW041902190726
13854UKWH00003B/1050